18143 EN
Australia: The Land Down Under

Meisel, Jacqueline Drobis
ATOS BL 6.3
Points: 1.0   MG

AUSTRALIA

The Land Down Under

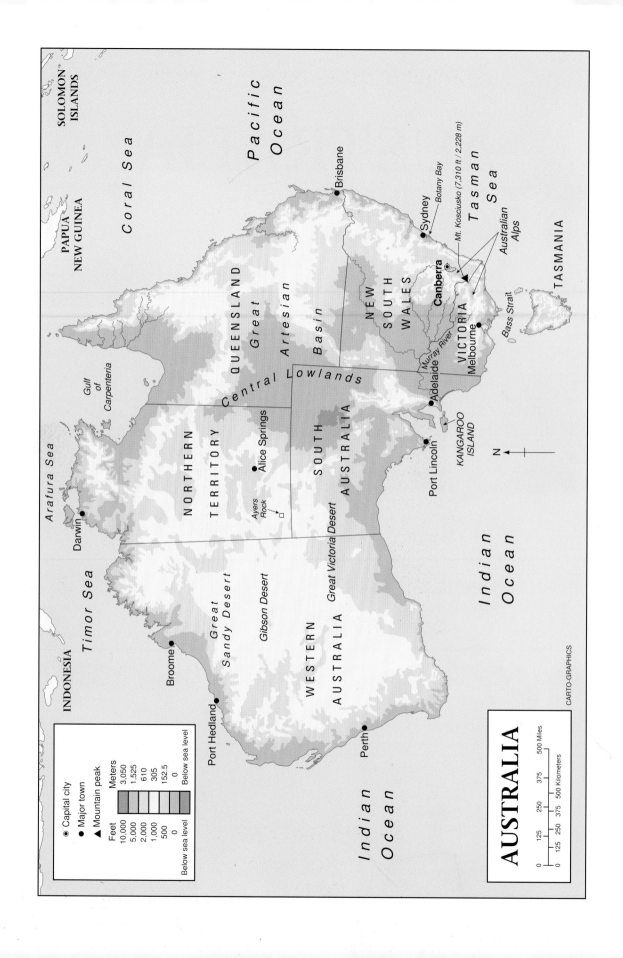

SOLOMON
ISLANDS

PAPUA
NEW GUINEA

INDONESIA

*Pacific
Ocean*

Coral Sea

*Tasman
Sea*

Brisbane

Sydney → *Botany Bay*

Mt. Kosciusko (7,310 ft / 2,228 m)

*Australian
Alps*

TASMANIA

Bass Strait

N E W
S O U T H
W A L E S

Canberra

VICTORIA

Melbourne

Murray River

Adelaide

KANGAROO
ISLAND

Port Lincoln

QUEENSLAND

*Great
Artesian
Basin*

Central Lowlands

S O U T H

A U S T R A L I A

*Gulf
of
Carpenteria*

Arafura Sea

Darwin

N O R T H E R N

T E R R I T O R Y

Alice Springs

*Ayers
Rock* □

Timor Sea

Broome

Port Hedland

*Great
Sandy Desert*

Gibson Desert

Great Victoria Desert

W E S T E R N

A U S T R A L I A

Perth

*Indian
Ocean*

*Indian
Ocean*

N

CARTO-GRAPHICS

AUSTRALIA

0	125	250	375	500 Miles
0	125	250	375	500 Kilometers

500 Kilometers

Capital city
Major town
▲ Mountain peak

Feet	Meters
10,000	3,050
5,000	1,525
2,000	610
1,000	305
500	152.5
0	0
Below sea level	Below sea level

EXPLORING CULTURES OF THE WORLD

AUSTRALIA

The Land Down Under

Jacqueline Drobis Meisel

BENCHMARK BOOKS

MARSHALL CAVENDISH
NEW YORK

With thanks to Dr. Henri Warmenhoven, Professor Emeritus of Political Science, Virginia Commonwealth University, for his expert review of the manuscript.

Benchmark Books
Marshall Cavendish Corporation
99 White Plains Road
Tarrytown, New York 10591-9001

© Marshall Cavendish Corporation 1997

Library of Congress Cataloging-in-Publication Data

Meisel, Jacqueline Drobis.
    Australia: the land down under / by Jacqueline Drobis Meisel.
        p.   cm. — (Exploring cultures of the world)
    Includes bibliographical references (p.).
    Summary: Discusses the history, landscape, people, and culture of the country of Australia.
    ISBN 0-7614-0139-3
    1. Australia—Juvenile literature.   [1. Australia.]   I. Title.   II. Series: Exploring cultures of the world (New York, N.Y.)
  DU96.D3   1997
  994—dc21

96-50163
CIP
AC

Printed in Hong Kong

Series design by Carol Matsuyama

Front cover: Young Aborigines in North Queensland
Back cover: Millstream National Park, western Australia

Photo Credits

Front cover and pages 15 (left), 30: ©John Cancalosi/Peter Arnold, Inc.; back cover and pages 11, 14 (top), 15 (right), 27–28: ©Australian Tourist Commission; title page and page 13: Chad Ehlers/International Stock Photo; page 6: ©Mark Newman/International Stock Photo; page 9: ©F. Dalgety/International Stock Photo; page 12: ©Johnny Stockshooter/International Stock Photo; page 14 (bottom): Anne B. Keiser/National Geographic Image Collection; page 16: ©Johan Elbers/International Stock Photo; page 18: ©North Wind Pictures; pages 19, 58: Tate Gallery, London/Art Resource, NY; page 21: Sam Abell/National Geographic Image Collection; page 24: ©Miwako Ikeda/International Stock Photo; pages 26, 42, 53: ©Fritz Prenzel/Peter Arnold, Inc.; page 32: ©Michael Ventura/Peter Arnold, Inc.; pages 34, 52: ©Frank Grant/International Stock Photo; page 36: Sam Abell/National Geographic Image Collection; page 39: William A. Allod/National Geographic Image Collection; page 41: Robert W. Madden/National Geographic Image Collection; page 44: ©Kelvin Aitken/Peter Arnold, Inc.; page 46: Robert W. Madden/National Geographic Image Collection; page 49: ©National Geographic Society; page 50: ©Chuck Szymanski/International Stock Photo; page 54: ©Giraudon/Art Resource, NY

Contents

This kangaroo drawn on a rock may have adorned the Australian landscape for thousands of years.

1
GEOGRAPHY AND HISTORY

Ancient Mysteries, Modern World

An Aboriginal Dreamtime Legend

A long time ago in the Dreamtime, when the world was made, there lived Kangaroo and Porpoise. They often went hunting far out in the bush.

Both Kangaroo and Porpoise had babies. One day, Kangaroo asked Porpoise to look after her baby while she went hunting for bush tucker, food found in the bush.

"All right," said Porpoise, "I'll look after him."

So Kangaroo went off on her own to look for some tasty long yams, goanna, and emu.

When Kangaroo came back, she said to Porpoise, "It's your turn now. You can go hunting and I'll look after your baby." So Porpoise went off in search of bush tucker and Kangaroo stayed behind to take care of the babies.

Porpoise was away for quite a long time, and her baby started crying because she was hungry. Porpoise heard her crying and rushed back to feed her. "Give me my baby," Porpoise said to Kangaroo. "She's hungry and I want to give her some milk."

But Kangaroo had decided she wanted to keep Porpoise's daughter for herself. "No!" said Kangaroo.

"She's crying for me," said Porpoise.

"No!" shouted Kangaroo.

"She's my daughter. Give her back!"

And so they argued. Kangaroo grabbed a stick and hit Porpoise, making a hole in her head. Porpoise got mad and grabbed a stick, too. She hit Kangaroo's arms. Now Kangaroo could not pick up her baby and could only hop away on her back legs.

Porpoise ran down to the beach and jumped into the water. She dived down and swam around for a while. When she came up, water spurted out of the hole in her head.

"I will stay like this forever," she said. "I'll live here in the sea." And she dived down again. Porpoise is still there today, playing in the water.

Next time you see a porpoise, look for a hole in its head. That is where Kangaroo hit Porpoise. And kangaroos still have little bent arms, from the time Porpoise hit Kangaroo with a stick. Although you can see a porpoise in many parts of the world, to see a kangaroo in its natural habitat, you will have to come to Australia.

The Country That Is a Continent

Australia is the only country in the world that is a continent. Since it is completely surrounded by water, it is also a very big island. It is often called the "Land Down Under" because it is located in the Southern Hemisphere of the earth. It is bordered on the west by the Indian Ocean and, on the east, by the South Pacific Ocean. Australia is an enormous country with plenty of space for its small population. Although mainland Australia is about as big as the continental United States, it is home to only 18 million people.

Australia is divided into eight governmental units: two territories and six states. The territories are called the Northern Territory and the Australian Capital Territory. The states are Queensland, New South Wales, Victoria, South Australia, Western Australia, and Tasmania. Tasmania is actually an island that lies to the southeast. A body of water called the Bass Strait separates the island from the mainland.

From the Great Sandy Desert to the Great Barrier Reef

Australia has three geographic regions: the Great Western Plateau, the Central Lowlands, and the Eastern Highlands. The Great Western Plateau is a dry, high, flat region that covers

Water pumped up from the ground by windmill power provides drinking water for these sheep in the parched outback.

two thirds of Australia. It is called the "outback." Few people live in this vast area. In the middle of the Great Western Plateau lie the Great Sandy Desert, the Gibson Desert, and the Great Victoria Desert. To the north and southwest of these deserts are hilly scrublands that can provide food for livestock, which are mostly sheep.

The Central Lowlands cover the mideastern part of the country. The region is too hot and dry to support crop farming. In the ground underneath these lowlands, though, lies the Great Artesian Basin. It provides vast natural reserves of water. Farmers pump the water to the surface using windmills. In this unusual way, the region is able to support a sheep industry.

The Eastern Highlands—sometimes called the Great Dividing Range—is a belt of raised land that stretches along the length of Australia's east coast. This region has low mountains, plateaus, and fertile coastal plains. The country's highest mountain is found here. Mount Kosciusko is only 7,310 feet (2,228 meters) high and rises from the Australian Alps.

The Eastern Highlands receive more rain than the rest of the country does. Most Australians live in this area.

The Great Barrier Reef is a long chain of living coral reefs and coral islands in the Pacific Ocean, close to Australia's northeast coast. This 1,200-mile-long (1,932-kilometer) wonder of nature is the largest deposit of coral in the world. Visitors can go snorkeling or scuba diving at the colorful reefs, walk near them at low tide, look at them through a glass-bottom boat, and fly over them in a low-flying airplane. The reefs are home to at least 400 kinds of brightly colored coral and about 1,500 varieties of fish and other marine life—some of them in colors as startling and beautiful as the coral.

The Great Barrier Reef is a beautiful but fragile natural environment.

To protect its coral and many rare species of wildlife, the Australian government made the Great Barrier Reef a national park. The park includes a bird sanctuary and a research center to help preserve this precious but fragile environment.

Sweet Water, Pleasant Climate

Much of Australia is hot, dry desert. Toward the east coast, where there is more rain, plant life increases. But throughout the country, the range of rainfall is enormous—from less than 6 inches (15 centimeters) each year in the deserts to more than 78 inches (198 centimeters) in tropical pockets in the north and in Tasmania's mountains.

Australians draw their water from natural basins, or bowls, beneath the earth's surface that collect and store water. They also have access to water from the Murray River and its tributaries, small rivers that branch off from the main river.

Technology and nature work together to provide water to this dry continent. The Snowy Mountains Scheme is a huge

11

Strange and wondrous stone forms dot a desert floor in western Australia.

project that sends freshwater from the mountains to the Murray River. The Snowy Mountains Scheme also produces electricity to power homes and businesses.

Most of northern Australia has a hot climate. The southern half of the continent is somewhat cooler, as it lies in the temperate, or mild, zone. Winters in the south can be cold, and the mountains receive heavy snowfalls, which are a treat for skiers.

Because Australia lies in the Southern Hemisphere, its seasons are the opposite of those in countries in the northern half of the world. Summer, for example, lasts from December to February.

Forest and Flowers

Although much of Australia is desert, there are many other environments as well. Desert changes to grasslands and then into woodlands. Close to the coast, the trees become thicker and taller, until there is true forest. There are even some pockets wet enough for rain forests to grow. And above the snowline, where no trees grow, there are meadows where rare and beautiful plants live.

Some of Australia's plant and animal species cannot be found anywhere else in the world. Since the continent lies so far from other lands, a number of plant and animal species have developed in isolation. Over time, these species became uniquely adapted to the Australian environment.

Australia is rich in plant species—there are more than 20,000 different kinds of plants. After the rare desert rainfalls, wildflowers spring up and change the landscape from dull brown to red, pink, blue, white, orange, and yellow. Australia's best-known tree, the eucalyptus (yoo-kah-LIP-tiss), also called a gum tree, and the acacia (ah-KAY-sha), also known as a wattle, grow in all regions except the driest deserts.

Triplet Falls, in southeastern Australia, helps water the lush rain forest.

Australia's Special Animals

Australia is home to some unique kinds of animals. Some of these are marsupials—mammals that give birth to young that still need more time to grow. They must be carried in their mother's pouch until they are ready to move about on their own.

The kangaroo is perhaps the best-known Australian marsupial. Kangaroos eat grass, seeds, and leaves. There are a great many kangaroos in Australia. Some people who live in rural areas, especially farmers and ranchers, think that these animals are a real problem. Kangaroos eat grass meant for sheep. They trample crops, and they hop

Some of Australia's special creatures: kangaroos with friends (below), the frill neck lizard (left).

The fierce little Tasmanian devil (above) and the gentle koala (right).

across country roads, often causing serious car wrecks.

The koala (koh-AH-lah) is another famous Australian marsupial. The word *koala* means "one who doesn't drink." Koalas get both their food and their water from simply eating the leaves of a certain kind of eucalyptus tree. Koalas are soft and gentle animals, and they make their homes in the trees.

Some other animals that live only in Australia are the Tasmanian devil, the duck-billed platypus, and the dingo. The Tasmanian devil is a small, fierce, meat-eater. It is strong enough to kill a sheep. The duck-billed platypus (PLAT-ah-puhs) is a very unusual animal. It has characteristics of both a mammal and a bird. It lays its eggs underwater, but it nurses its young. The dingo, a wild dog, preys mainly on small mammals, but when they are scarce, it will attack sheep, cattle, and kangaroos. It is a mean-looking animal with a frightening howl.

There are also some birds that are found only in Australia. The kookaburra (koo-kah-BUH-rah) and the emu (EE-moo) are among them. The kookaburra is a gray-brown bird that dwells in the woodlands. It is sometimes called the "bush-man's clock" because its call can be heard very early in the morning and just after sunset. The kookaburra can eat venomous snakes and has a strange call that sounds like fiendish laughter.

Emus look similar to ostriches and, like ostriches, cannot fly. They have thin legs, fat bodies, and long, thin necks. Emus are sociable creatures that walk around the rural inland areas in flocks, searching for fruits and insects.

The First Australians

Australia's first people, the Aborigines (ah-buh-RI-juh-nees), are believed to have come to the continent from southeast Asia at least 40,000 years ago. The name comes from the Latin

These Aborigines, wearing body paint for a sacred ceremony, have a long and rich cultural tradition.

ab origine, which means "from the beginning." The Aborigines probably traveled on rafts between islands that are now covered by water.

Eventually, there were some 500 Aboriginal groups and 200 Aboriginal languages. Before 1788, when settlers from Europe arrived, there were about 350,000 Aborigines. They had all of the land of Australia to themselves.

The people were nomadic—they moved from place to place and did not build permanent homes for themselves. The women gathered roots, berries, and seeds, and hunted small animals. The men hunted larger animals. The Aborigines made tools from materials that they gathered. For example, by chipping stones, they were able to make sharp edges for cutting skins.

Colonization and Convicts

For many years, Europeans suspected that there was a vast land in the south. They thought that it was needed to balance the large land masses in the Northern Hemisphere, so that the world would not tip over! Mapmakers called this mysterious place *Terra Australis Incognita*. In Latin, *terra* means "land;" *australis* means "southern;" and *incognita* means "unknown"—Unknown Southern Land.

In the 1600s, Dutch merchants and explorers landed on the north and west coasts of Australia. The British heard the Dutch reports about these places and were interested in the land for themselves—but only if they could find gold or trade goods there. A British explorer and pirate, William Dampier, scouted Australia's west coast. But he left, believing the land to be of no value. For a while, the British lost interest in the big continent.

The explorations of Captain James Cook eventually led the British to establish colonies in Australia.

Then, on April 19, 1770, Captain James Cook, exploring for the British Navy, reached Botany Bay in his ship, the *Endeavor*. Cook claimed the eastern half of Australia for the king of England. The Aborigines, however, had been living there for thousands of years before the arrival of Captain Cook. They considered Australia to be *their* land.

It took the British some years to decide to establish a colony in Australia. England was experiencing terrible social problems. Its cities, especially London, had many people without jobs. These poor people lived in slums—dirty, overcrowded neighborhoods.

Widespread crime added to these problems. Harsh laws sent people to prison for a long time for even minor crimes. So many people were imprisoned that the jails became horribly overcrowded with men, women, and even children. Disease spread quickly because conditions were so bad. Something had to be done to improve this situation.

The British government decided to reduce the overcrowding in jails by "transportation"—sending convicted criminals, called convicts, to Australia. In 1788, the first British settlers arrived after an eight-month sea voyage. At Sydney Harbor, they established the British colony of New South Wales. About three quarters of the 1,000 passengers were convicts.

At first, life was very hard for the new settlers. When they arrived, they found that the seeds they had brought for planting were damaged. To make matters worse, the soil was poor and crops did not do well. Their cattle and sheep died or escaped. Some were taken by the Aborigines.

Conditions slowly improved, however, and the colony grew. As the colony established itself, more free settlers began to arrive, but the British continued to send convicts. About 160,000 British convicts were sent to Australia between 1788 and 1868. Some were treated very cruelly. Eventually, in 1868, the transportation of convicts from England ended.

The British raise the flag over their colony of New South Wales, founded in 1788.

Creating Order Out of Chaos

In the early years, the British colony was very chaotic. Laws were unclear. When Lachlan Macquarie became governor of the colony of New South Wales in 1810, order came at last. Macquarie established Australia's first bank and money systems. He had roads and public buildings constructed. He helped former convicts to become productive citizens after they had served their prison terms. Macquarie also encouraged more settlement to the west. Exploration and expansion soon got under way.

Colonial Expansion

While conditions improved for white settlers, they grew worse for the Aborigines. The British helped themselves to huge pieces of land west of the Eastern Highlands. They used guns to chase away or kill the native people. The new settlers also competed with the Aborigines for food, such as fish. They drove away kangaroos. Slowly, the Aboriginal population disappeared from the region.

Meanwhile, Europeans continued to arrive in Australia. Free settlers (not convicts) traveled to Australia in search of new opportunities for making a living. Some settlers were attracted by the broad expanses of land in the west. Even though much of it was dry, it was free. Most landholders began raising Merino sheep, a breed that was brought over from Spain. Merinos had very soft fleeces and could survive on dry vegetation. These sheep produced a fine wool that was soon being sold to Europe. Camels from Afghanistan were important to Australia's build-up, too. Before good roads were built, these strong animals carried supplies.

European settlers started the sheep-raising industry in Australia. Today, products from sheep, such as wool and mutton, are an important part of the country's economy.

While most people were happy to stay in one place, others were more adventurous. They went on dangerous journeys of discovery along the coast and into the harsh interior, helping to pave the way for new colonies.

At first, there had been just the single colony of New South Wales. Soon other British colonies sprang up. Each colony had its own governor, appointed by the British government, and its own laws and police. By 1829, the British claimed the western part of the continent of Australia as their own.

The different colonies did not get along very well. Soon they would have to figure out a way to work together.

A Golden Surprise

The discovery of gold in Bathurst, west of Sydney, in 1851 led to many changes in Australian society. Until that time, sheep farming had been the continent's most important industry. But with 18 million sheep and only 400,000 settlers, there had never been enough people to do all the work. Suddenly, Australia had no trouble attracting settlers. Immigrants poured in from around the world. The gold rush helped boost the population past 1 million by 1860. With so many more people, there were more workers, so large landholders did not need convict labor anymore.

Strength in Unity

The colonies finally decided to put aside their differences and cooperate. They formed a union called a federation. Under this system, the national government would have most powers, but the colonies—now known as states—would keep some authority. Queen Victoria, the queen of England, announced that Australia would be given status as a nation on January 1, 1901. Australia became a "commonwealth" within the British Empire. This meant that England would handle Australia's foreign affairs and that laws passed in England would be more important than laws made in Australia.

As a result of this political status, Australia was automatically at war when Great Britain declared war on Germany in 1914. More than 330,000 Australian soldiers were sent to Europe and North Africa to fight in World War I (1914–1918). About 60,000 Australians were killed—an enormous number for a nation with such a small population.

After the war, European immigration to Australia continued. For a while, the standard of living improved for

Australians. They made money from manufacturing and selling wool, minerals, and food to other countries. Australia's cities, spaced so far apart, now had the money to build more roads and railroads.

But the Great Depression hit the world in the 1930s. It meant hard times for Australians as well. One third of the working people lost their jobs. Immigration stopped.

In 1939, Great Britain was at war again. Its enemies were Germany and Italy, and, a little later, Japan. During World War II (1939–1945), Australia again helped Great Britain by sending soldiers to Europe and North Africa. But, this time, Australia itself was in danger—from Japan.

Japanese aircraft bombed the Australian cities of Darwin and Broome in early 1942. Since the British were involved in fighting the Germans in Europe, Australia turned to the United States for help. American soldiers moved in to fight with the Australians against the Japanese. Finally, in August 1945, Japan surrendered. Meanwhile, the Americans and the Australians had begun a lasting friendship.

Progress and Prosperity

After World War II, there was a great deal of economic growth around the world. The countries that had suffered during the terrible war were rebuilding. They needed the raw materials and agricultural products that Australia could supply. What Australia did not have, however, was labor—people to do the work.

To encourage people to settle in Australia, the government offered free land and help with travel expenses. Two million immigrants, mostly from southern Europe, arrived in the 1950s and 1960s. Soon there were new languages to be

A sleek monorail train system snakes through modern downtown Sydney.

AUSTRALIAN GOVERNMENT

Australia is made up of a federation of states, like the United States. It is run as a parliamentary democracy. The country is sometimes called a constitutional monarchy because the king or queen of Britain is also the monarch of Australia. The British monarch is represented in Australia by a governor-general and by six state governors. However, Australia makes its own decisions and has its own constitution.

The country has governments at the federal, state, and local levels. The federal government is in charge of things affecting the entire country, like defense, income tax, immigration, and social security. Each state government is responsible for running its schools and hospitals and maintaining its police force. Cities and shires, or counties, are governed by local councils headed by a mayor. They make decisions affecting local matters, such as town planning.

The federal Parliament is made up of two groups: the House of Representatives and the Senate. The House, which makes laws, has 148 members, who are elected every three years. Its proposed laws, however, must be passed by a majority in the Senate. Each state has twelve senators. They are elected to six-year terms.

The political party that has the majority of members in the House of Representatives runs the government. That party chooses the prime minister and the cabinet from its membership. Citizens over the age of eighteen are required by law to vote.

The Australian judicial system is similar to that of the United States. Each state has its own system of courts. There is also a national court system, overseen by the High Court.

heard, interesting foods to be tasted, different customs to learn about, and useful work skills to offer—all in Australia.

In the 1970s, world demand for Australia's main products dropped. Australians realized that their farming and mining industries would not be enough to help them keep their high standard of living. Since then, they have been working to create a wider variety of products to sell to other countries. In recent years, more and more tourists have been coming to Australia. Tourism is now an important industry.

These young Aborigine men have painted themselves in preparation for a traditional ceremony of music and dance.

2
THE PEOPLE

The Australian Way

The Aborigines

For many thousands of years, the Aborigines were the only inhabitants on the Australian continent. The land was the focus of their existence. They knew all about edible plants, ways to fish, and how to stalk and kill animals for food. They did not plant crops or raise animals for food.

Each Aboriginal group had its own area, or territory, within which it moved with the changing seasons. As they looked for food and water, the people carried digging sticks, food bags, and didgeridoos (dee-jer-ree-DOOZ)—musical instruments that make a wailing sound. They also carried hunting weapons, including boomerangs, wooden spears, and stone axes.

There never was one, united Aboriginal nation in Australia. The 500 small groups were organized along family lines. Often they got along with one another. Sometimes they fought over the best camping areas and water sources. Each group had its own language, but they all shared certain customs, such as strict family values. For example, the young and strong members of the group provided for the old and the weak.

The Dreamtime

All Aborigines shared the belief that the land is sacred. They also believed in the dreamtime. This was the time when the spirits created the world and gave it life. The spirits then went to live in certain trees and rocks. These trees and rocks are holy to the Aborigines. Ayers Rock, called Uluru (oo-lah-ROO) by Aborigines, in the center of Australia, is believed to be the origin of all things.

Ayers Rock, which rises starkly from the flat desert, is a sacred place to the Aborigines, who call it Uluru.

Aboriginal religion makes it possible to enter the dream-time by going into a trance, or a state of dreaming. A shaman, or priest, will endure painful physical ceremonies to go into a trance. Then, after he enters the dreamtime, he will exchange thoughts with the spirits of the ancestors. Later, he will recite his people's legends, show the legends through dance, or make rock paintings. In these ways, Aborigines have passed dreamtime stories from generation to generation.

Modern Times

Not many Aborigines continue to live in the old ways. Today, most live in or around towns and cities. But they are not fully accepted, and they are the poorest Australians. Only about 200,000 Aborigines are left in Australia. Many of their ancestors were killed by diseases brought from Europe, like cholera and smallpox. They were chased away from their traditional hunting grounds by settlers with guns, so they starved. They were sometimes even rounded up and killed because the white settlers wanted them out of a particular area in order to build a ranch or a farm.

These children will grow up proud of their Aboriginal heritage.

For many years, the government in Australia tried to make the Aborigines more like the Europeans. Now, however, the government has come to believe that this attitude caused most of the problems in the first place. A new pride in traditional Aboriginal culture is beginning to grow.

Today, there are programs that encourage Aborigines to learn about and keep their unique culture. Helpful people called "land rights activists" have been working to give back the land areas that first belonged to the Aborigines. In some preschools, Aboriginal children learn about their culture. In areas with lots of Aboriginal students, courses are taught in both Aboriginal languages and in English.

Better medical care, legal help, and economic assistance are now being provided by the Australian government. Other programs have been started to help Aborigines support themselves or start their own small businesses.

The "New Australians"

Since World War II, hundreds of thousands of Italians, Greeks, Germans, Dutch, and other Europeans were made welcome in Australia. These people brought useful skills and trades. They helped to build factories, mines, and roads.

Freedom of religion is protected by Australia's constitution. For the most part, the many religions of the "new Australians" are accepted. In fact, immigrants are encouraged to keep their own cultures and religious practices.

The Australian-born children of those immigrants—the second generation—usually speak English. And while they may follow their parents' traditions and religion, they still think of themselves as Australians first.

Asian Australians

In the 1850s, during the gold rush, many Chinese people arrived. The Australians were prejudiced against them because they were of a different race. The "White Australian Policy" was created to keep out everyone who was not white, or Caucasian. Asians were not allowed to settle in Australia between 1901 and 1973, when this law was finally changed.

After the law was changed, many Asians arrived from India, the Philippines, Japan, China, and Hong Kong. Some opened small businesses, such as restaurants and hardware

This Buddhist temple is a peaceful spot in the bustling city of Sydney.

stores. Others found work in the areas of science, computers, and technology. These fields will be of great importance to the country in the coming years.

Australia has also taken in many Asian refugees, people who have had to leave their countries because of war or other political troubles. These include people from Vietnam, Laos, and Cambodia. Like the other "new Australians," Asian Australians are allowed freedom of religion. Many Asian communities have built places of worship, such as Buddhist temples.

Bustling Cities

Australia's most important cities are on the east coast—except for Canberra, the capital, which lies inland in the southeastern part of the country. Sydney is Australia's largest and most modern city, with a population of 3.6 million. Its long port on the southeastern coast reaches inland for 13 miles (20 kilometers). The harbor attracted Captain Cook many years ago, and it continues to be a focus of commerce. Ships come and go, taking Australia's products to foreign markets and bringing in items that Australians need. People who work in Sydney are teachers and doctors, government workers and shopkeepers—doing the kinds of jobs you would expect to find in a big, modern city. Sydney has three universities.

Melbourne is Australia's second-largest city and is the capital of the state of Victoria. Just over 3 million people live there. Melbourne grew very quickly after gold was discovered in Victoria in the 1850s. It is a quieter city than Sydney. Yet

SAY IT IN AUSTRALIAN ENGLISH

Although English is the official language of Australia, you might need some help translating Australia's unusual and widely used slang.

barbie	barbecue
billy	a tin can used to boil water for tea over an open fire out in the bush. A tea kettle is also called a billy.
bloke	a man (guy or fellow)
crook	broken or sick, as in, "My bike is crook. It needs a new chain."
flog	to sell
Good on ya!	Good for you!
mate	your good friend, or buddy
nipper	a young child
Oz	Australia; people who live in Oz are Aussies.
postie	postman (mail carrier)
She'll be apples.	It will be all right.
uni	university
walkabout	to wander

it also offers many cultural opportunities. There are three universities in Melbourne as well as museums, theaters, and medical and scientific research institutions. The city, with its British atmosphere, is known for its lovely parks and gardens and its beautiful old buildings.

Perth is the only major city on the west coast of Australia, on the Indian Ocean. Between Perth and its closest major neighboring city, Adelaide, lie about 1,500 miles (2,400 kilometers), mostly desert. Over 1 million people live in Perth, and it is growing quickly. The city's industry centers around mining and processing such resources as diamonds, oil, and iron ore.

Electric trains carry passengers up and down this gaily decorated Melbourne street.

The name of the capital of Australia, *Canberra*, is an Aboriginal word meaning "meeting place." Canberra is not part of any of the six states. Instead, it is situated in the Australian Capital Territory (ACT). This is similar to how, in the United States, the capital, Washington, is located in the District of Columbia. Canberra is a city of government offices.

The Wide-Open Outback

Outback life is very different from city life. The outback has great expanses of dry, open land and very few people. Huge distances separate places. Many of the people who live and work in the "Great Empty," as some people call the outback, have come to appreciate its silent beauty.

But outback living is not all peace and quiet. It also involves hard work. Sheep ranchers work from early in the morning until sunset in certain seasons. At sheep-shearing time, they work late into the night.

Another demanding job is opal mining. Workers have to dig underground, then sift through the soil for the precious gemstones. Hard work and good luck sometimes pay off when a miner finds a gem worth thousands of dollars.

Outback living can be dangerous. Weather, especially rainfall, is unpredictable. Homesteads are linked by two-way radio so that residents can share information about road conditions and wildfire warnings. Motor vehicles have to be well taken care of and equipped with extra water, gasoline, and spare parts. To break down in the desert of the Great Empty in the heat of summer can be fatal. In each outback region, there is a homestead with a landing strip. This allows the Royal Flying Doctor Service to land its planes in case of a medical emergency.

Mom, Dad, and the kids at their homestead in the outback

3
FAMILY LIFE, FESTIVALS, AND FOOD

Time for Family and Friends

Family and friends are very important to Australians. Both their history and geography help to explain why they cherish a close and supportive family and community. In the early years of the colony, the settlers were very far away from their homes and extended families in Great Britain. In those days, there were no telephones to connect them to the outside world. It was before there were airplanes to take them back home if they did not like what they found Down Under. They simply had to stay put and make the best of it. They were faced with matters of life and death—surviving in their harsh new land. Neighbors helped one another to build houses, plant gardens for food, nurse children through sickness, bury people who died. Small, close-knit communities of friends helped cheer up those who were sad and homesick. This friendly spirit continues in the Australian character today.

For Aborigines, the importance of close family ties stems from thousands of years of outback living, which some still follow today. In this traditional lifestyle, survival depends upon cooperation, sharing food, and helping one another in times of need.

Families, City Style

Life for most Australian families in the cities is not too different from family life in North America and Europe. Australians live in nuclear families, made up of parents, brothers, and sisters. Some people from non-British cultures, however, share one big house with their extended families, which include grandparents, aunts, uncles, and cousins.

Most Australian families live in houses, not apartments. During the week, family members get up at 6:30 or 7:00 A.M. and eat a breakfast of eggs and toast or cereal, with juice or coffee. Children attend school from about 9:00 A.M. to 3:30 P.M. Adults usually work from 9:00 A.M. to 5:00 P.M. Family members eat dinner together. Then the children do their homework while the parents do hobbies or chores, or watch television.

On weekends, Australians often play their favorite sport or watch a game. Backyard or beach barbecues are very popular. The weekend is also a time to take a drive and visit grandparents and other relatives. Other activities include attending parties; visiting the zoo; going to the ballet, the symphony, or a rock concert; and eating out.

Living in the Great Empty

Life in the outback is quieter than life in the cities. It is often difficult, although modern conveniences make it more comfortable than in the past. Sheep stations (ranches) and farms may be thousands of acres in size, so it can be quite a jaunt just to visit neighbors. Trips to town may happen just once a week.

The farm or ranch house is usually very big. It has to provide space for the ranch office, for a study or classroom, if necessary, and for a guest room to put up overnight visitors. The house also needs a large storeroom and pantry, because the family must stock up on plenty of food and supplies. Chickens and cows on the farm provide fresh eggs and milk, and the family garden provides fresh vegetables.

Ranch families must find their own entertainment. Many of them have swimming pools. They may also have a variety of board games as well as table tennis and pool. Although they do have television, they don't have many channels. VCRs and videotapes help to provide entertainment.

There are lots of opportunities for fun in the vast countryside. Some people enjoy fishing and hunting. Horseback riding is very popular, as are motorcycles. A few families may get together and go camping or have a barbecue. There are not many opportunities for people to socialize, so gatherings like these are thoroughly enjoyed, especially by the children.

Family members enjoy a game of cricket.

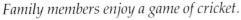

Home Sweet Home

The Australian dream is for each family to have its own separate house. That dream is a reality for most Australians—three out of four families own their own homes. There are not many apartment buildings.

Australian houses are roomy and comfortable. The most important room is the living room, or lounge, which is big. This is the gathering place for family and friends. In the lounge, children usually do their homework, the parents drink tea, and the family watches television.

Holiday Time

Australians know how to have fun. There are plenty of holidays and festivals on the Australian calendar.

January 1 is New Year's Day. New Year's Eve is celebrated with special dinners, dances, and champagne at midnight for the adults. New Year's Day is a time for making New Year's resolutions and starting life afresh.

Two Australia-only days are observed: Australia Day and ANZAC Day. (ANZAC is short for Australian and New Zealand Army Corps.) Australia Day is a happy time celebrated on January 26. It commemorates the arrival of the first British settlers. On this day, the landing at Sydney Harbor is reenacted, and children dress up in historical costumes. Concerts and sports events take place, and fireworks displays light up the night sky.

ANZAC Day, which occurs on April 25, is a solemn occasion. It is a day to remember the many soldiers who fought and died overseas for Australia and for England. War veterans in uniform take part in parades and make speeches in honor of their fallen comrades.

In the annual Australian Day parade in Sydney, people wear colonial costumes.

The birthday of Elizabeth II, queen of England, is also a public holiday. In most of Australia it is celebrated on the second Monday in June, even though the queen's actual birthday is April 21. On this holiday, family and friends gather for food and fun.

Easter is celebrated according to the church calendar, usually in March or April, which, in Australia, is in the autumn. It is an important religious holiday for Christians. Good Friday and Easter Monday are official holidays. Some people attend church services, and Australian children enjoy Easter-egg hunts.

Christmas, December 25, is a time of Nativity plays, the singing of carols, and gift-giving. Christmas occurs during the hot Australian summer, so lunch may be a backyard barbecue or a picnic at the beach.

The day after Christmas is known as Boxing Day, a day celebrated in the British Commonwealth countries. It was established back in the days when people would put their

A woman performs a traditional Japanese dance at the Japan Festival.

Christmas leftovers into boxes for the poor. These days, workers such as mail carriers and the newspaper-delivery boy or girl are given a tip or a small gift. Shops are open on Boxing Day, and the after-Christmas sales draw bargain hunters.

Australians who do not follow the Christian faith celebrate their own religious holidays throughout the year. The Chinese New Year is a time for Chinese families and friends to gather together and enjoy food and entertainment. On this day, they settle debts and start anew. Jews observe the major Jewish holidays. These are Rosh Hashanah, Yom Kippur, and Passover. The month-long, dawn-to-dusk fast of Ramadan is one of the most important holidays that Muslims observe.

Festivals

Australia's cities draw large crowds at festival time. Adelaide holds the Festival of the Arts every even-numbered year, such as 1996. Artists, musicians, and performers take part in plays, street performances, and exhibitions. The Melbourne Festival, also called the Moomba Festival, is held each year. *Moomba* is an Aboriginal word that means "Let's get together and have fun!" It is held during the first two weeks of March.

Hundreds of events are on the Moomba festival calendar, which ends in a big procession of floats. The Sydney Festival is also held each year. It is famous for free outdoor performances by the Sydney Symphony Orchestra and the Australia Opera Company.

The traditional festivals of the Aborigines are called corroboree (kuh-RO-buh-ree). These are sacred ceremonies of music and dance. Dancers paint dreamtime symbols on their bodies and are led by musicians who play the didgeridoo and beat clap-sticks. Men take the main roles at corroboree.

Corroboree are held for different reasons. Sometimes the people may be asking for relief from drought or danger. Sometimes they may be honoring the guardian spirits. The sacred ceremony is private and open only to members of that particular group of Aborigines. A feast is served after corroboree.

Put Another Shrimp on the Barbie!

In the cities, many different kinds of foods can be enjoyed. The variety of restaurants is endless—Chinese, Japanese, Italian, Greek, Lebanese, French, Danish, Indian, Indonesian, and Russian. Hearty English food, though, has had the greatest influence on Australian taste. The basic meal for Australians of British or other Commonwealth background is built around meat, potatoes, and one or two vegetables. English meat pies are very popular and can be found in most fast-food restaurants.

Australians tend to eat more red meat than people of other nations, especially lamb, because of the many sheep farms. Health-conscious people are starting to cut down on the amount of red meat they eat. They are eating more salads, vegetables, and pasta.

Australians have perfected the fine art of the barbecue. Meat and fish are grilled over the fire, and salad and bread are plentiful. Australian beer, wines, and soft drinks are served well chilled. For dessert, there might be lamingtons—sponge-cake squares covered with chocolate and coconut—or pavlova, a smooth meringue shell filled with whipped cream and fruit.

"Bush tucker" is a more ancient tradition than the barbecue. It is a meal eaten out in the bush. Bush tucker—eaten for thousands of years by the Aborigines—includes any edible plants and animals found in the outback.

Examples of bush tucker are fat, white slugs called "witchetty," grubs (insect larvae, eaten raw), wild bees, and wild grasses. Traditionally, most small animals and insects are

Aquaculturists raise fish and other creatures of the sea to meet the demand for seafood in Australia. This aquaculture farmer on Kangaroo Island raises freshwater crayfish.

Pavlova Meringue Fruit Dessert

4 egg whites, at room temperature
1/2 teaspoon salt
1 cup sugar

2 teaspoons cornstarch
2 teaspoons apple cider vinegar
3 cups whipped cream
4 fresh kiwi

1. Preheat oven to 300° F. Place an 8-inch pie pan or plate upside down on a greased and floured cookie sheet. Trace around it with your clean fingertip to mark a circle in the flour.

2. Put egg whites and salt in mixing bowl. Whip into soft peaks. Add sugar, a little at a time, beating after each addition until the whites are smooth and glossy and hold stiff peaks.

3. In a small bowl, mix cornstarch and vinegar until smooth. Use a spatula to fold this mixture very gently (do not stir) into the egg whites until well blended. Pour whites into center of circle marked on cookie sheet. Spread meringue evenly to edges of circle.

4. Place on middle shelf in oven. Reduce oven heat to 250°F. Bake until outside of meringue is firm and pale tan in color, about 1 hour. Cool for 15 minutes. Carefully remove from cookie sheet. Let stand at room temperature until ready to serve. Do not cover or chill.

To serve, spread top and sides with whipped cream and decorate with slices of kiwi. Serves 8.

eaten raw. Larger animals are roasted over hot coals. These days, in specialty restaurants, adventurous eaters can try kangaroo-tail soup and crocodile steaks.

Damper bread and billy tea are an essential part of a bush picnic. Damper is made from wheat flour mixed with water and kneaded. The dough is placed in a cast-iron pot in a hole in the ground and covered with hot coals to bake. A hard, black crust forms when it is ready. Eaten with plenty of golden syrup, it should be washed down with billy tea. This is made from a handful of loose tea leaves thrown into a tin can in which water has been boiled over an open flame.

These Australian schoolboys attend a boarding school together.

4

SCHOOL AND RECREATION

Learning and Playing Down Under

Nearly everyone in Australia can read and write, thanks to the country's excellent school system. Most children who live in towns and cities leave their houses after breakfast and go to school until it is time to come home in the late afternoon. However, children in the outback often do not get to sit at a desk in a classroom with a group of schoolmates. Their schooling happens right at home on the ranch, by way of the radio, television, computer e-mail, and regular mail. Other outback children go to boarding schools.

All children between the ages of six and fifteen must attend school. Many schoolchildren wear uniforms. Where uniforms are not required, dress codes must be followed.

The School System
The Australian school system is loosely based on the British system. In Australia, the first grade is called "year one." Elementary school is known as "primary school." Primary

schools go from year one through year six or seven, depending on the area. Children in primary school are between five and twelve years of age. The main focus of primary school is to teach every child to read and write, to do arithmetic, and to learn something about history and simple science.

After primary school, students go on to secondary school, which is divided into junior secondary (ages thirteen to sixteen) and secondary (ages sixteen to eighteen). In the last two years of school, students who plan to enter college study hard for an important entrance exam.

SCHOOL OF THE AIR

Children who live on isolated sheep stations and farms in the outback are too far away from town to get to school every day. Homes usually have a small room that serves as a classroom. Here you would probably find a desk, a bookshelf filled with books, maps on the wall, possibly a chalkboard, a two-way radio, and maybe a computer.

These children are taught their lessons in several ways. A radio teacher may talk to a few children on different farms at the same time by a two-way radio. "Two-way" means that the teacher can talk and can also hear the children answer questions. Their voices are transmitted over the airwaves, which is why this is popularly called School of the Air. Some lessons appear on television; after watching the program, the students must answer questions about it in a workbook. Some children also have tutors. Often this is a parent. But sometimes a qualified teacher looking for a taste of life in the Great Empty is hired.

At least once a month, outback children attend school in the nearest town for a day. This gives them a chance to get used to being in a classroom and to play with other children of their age. By the time they are ready for secondary school, most of these outback students will make a daily trip to town. Some will stay in town during the week to attend boarding school.

Computers are useful to Australian children both in and out of school.

Education is free at government, or public, schools. About 80 percent of Australian children attend public schools. The rest go to private schools, usually connected with a religious group—Protestant, Roman Catholic, or Jewish.

In Australia, children are encouraged to ask questions. They are discouraged from simply learning facts by rote and accepting what they read in their textbooks. Teachers believe this kind of learning helps students to think better and make them better prepared to solve problems.

Free Time: Time for Fun

After school, there are lots of things for children to do in the cities and towns. They can choose from a wide range of sports, band, and drama clubs to fill their afternoons. The cities also

Australians love the seashore. The beaches near the cities are often crowded with swimmers and surfers.

offer many libraries, museums, and parks, where children can enjoy some quiet time. There is also the beach. In addition to swimming, Australians love to play volleyball on the sand and go surfing.

For the child who lives on a remote sheep station, the end of the morning's lessons is not the end of his or her "workday." There are always some chores to be done around the ranch house and its gardens. You might find a child feeding chickens or digging up some vegetables for dinner. Once school and work are out of the way, the youngster in the Great Empty might saddle up a horse and go for a ride under the wide blue sky. Or he might go swimming in the ranch pool.

Sporting Pastimes

Australians are serious about their sports. They love to watch and they love to play. Besides hiking, boating, fishing, cycling, and horseback riding, there are favorite organized sports.

Cricket, played from October to March, is the most popular summertime sport in Australia. Cricket was introduced by the British. Teams from every state but Tasmania play each other twice during the season for the Sheffield Shield, Australia's top cricket prize. Cricket matches are played against England and other countries that were once part of the British Empire. The required dress is all white—white long pants, a white shirt, and white shoes. Each team has a cap in its club colors. The sport is played almost entirely by men. There are few women's cricket teams.

Cricket is played with a wooden bat and a small, hard ball. There are two wickets. A wicket is made up of three upright wooden sticks with a wooden strip across the top of the sticks. Although both cricket and baseball are played with a bat and a ball, the sports do not have much in common.

Australians love to *watch* cricket, but they love to *play* tennis. The country has produced quite a few world-class tennis champions. These include Rod Laver, Pat Cash, Evonne

Goolagong Cawley, and John Newcombe. The Australian Open, held in the state of Victoria, is one of the four Grand Slam international events that attract the best players from all over the world.

During the winter months, Australia's sports calendar is devoted to rugby, which is called "football" or "footie." It is played three different ways: Rugby Union, Rugby League, and Australian Rules. The first two are very similar to each

Rugby is played three different ways Down Under. Australian Rules rugby is the most popular version.

These men in Alice Springs, in central Australia, play polo with a twist—on camels.

other. The third, Australian Rules, is the most popular form of the game. The game first began in Melbourne in the 1800s. It is still enthusiastically followed there by thousands of fans.

Australians are very talented at other sports as well. Some enjoy playing polo, a game played on horseback. One of the best golfers in the world is Greg Norman, who was raised in Queensland. Australians have also done very well competing internationally at swimming, soccer, yacht racing, surfing, and Formula One car racing.

Malangi de Milingimbi, an Aborigine, uses ancient symbols and shapes in this painting of a funeral ceremony.

5
THE ARTS

Something for Everyone

Australia offers something for everyone when it comes to the arts. From a fancy production at the Sydney Opera House to the haunting wail of a didgeridoo, you are sure to find music, art, or dance that you enjoy.

Dreamtime Art and Music

The corroboree, the sacred ceremony of the Aborigines, mixes the spiritual and the artistic. Music, dance, painting, story-telling, and prayer all come together in one ceremony.

Aboriginal artists continue traditions that are tens of thousands of years old. They paint certain symbols on tree branches, in the sand, on their bodies, on cave walls, and on canvas. Each symbol, or design, has a specific meaning. This is important because the Aborigines have an oral tradition. They mostly tell stories and sing songs to pass on information from one generation to the next. They have not written things down to record them. The painted symbols are almost like a form of writing.

However, some Aboriginal artists, like the late Albert Namatjira, have created new artistic styles. These are a blend of ancient symbolic painting and modern art techniques.

A few Aboriginal writers, like the poet Oodgeroo Noonuccal (formerly Kath Walker), are doing the same sort of thing with their work. They are creating new works from beautiful old Aboriginal poems, songs, myths, and legends.

The Classics

For a long time, you could not tell the difference between a painting done by a European and one done by an Australian. In the late 1800s, for instance, Australian painters were strongly influenced by French artists. Over time, however, a truly Australian art developed. Eventually, the Australian Impressionists, such as Frederick McCubbin and Tom Roberts, managed to capture a unique Australian feeling in their paintings.

Australia's major cities have a number of fine art museums and galleries that display the best and most interesting of the country's painting, sculpture, pottery, and photography. The Australian National Gallery, in Canberra, for example, is famous for its collection of Aboriginal art.

Classical music is also appreciated in Australia. In order to reach a wider audience, however, Australia's best performers must travel to Europe and the United States. Soprano Joan Sutherland, a world-famous opera star, was born and raised in Australia. Guitarist John Williams is also Australian and so was composer Percy Grainger.

The striking Sydney Opera House, completed in 1973, is proof of Australians' love of live performance. The Opera House looks like an enormous piece of sculpture, like a ship's sails billowing in the wind, shimmering just above the water of Sydney Harbor.

The Written Word

British settlers began writing about life in Australia right from the start. There are diaries, letters, poems, articles, and stories that trace the experience of settling into a strange, new land. Many Australian short stories and novels are set in the Great Empty, perhaps because it is easier to pay close attention to individual human beings and their relationships when they are so isolated. On the other hand, living in remote areas can make for some very funny tales about weird outback characters!

Famous writers from the last century include Miles Franklin. Her novel *My Brilliant Career* was made into a movie starring Australian film star Judy Davis. Henry Lawson is also very important to Australian literature. He wrote mainly in the early part of this century and is best known for his bush stories and his poetry. Lawson's characters are true to life and very funny.

One of Australia's best short-story writers and novelists was Katharine Susannah Prichard, who died in 1969. Her stories often have a deep political meaning. They make the reader think about why certain people have political power and why others do not.

Moving to more recent times, if you know of the award-winning film *Schindler's List*, then you are already familiar with the work of Thomas Keneally. An Australian, Keneally

AUSTRALIA IN ARTS AND LETTERS

Percy Grainger (1882–1961) was a pianist and composer who experimented with electronic music long before it became popular. He made frequent use of folk tunes and is known for his *Children's March*.

Patrick White (1912–1990), an author whose novels contain complex symbols and myths. He won the Nobel Prize for Literature in 1973 for *The Eye of the Storm*. He also wrote *Rider in the Chariot* and *Voss*. *Voss* was made into an opera by composer Richard Meale.

Sir Sidney Nolan (1917–1992) was an influential artist who captured the essence of the Australian character and landscape on canvas. His best-known works are the Ned Kelly series, from the 1940s to the 1950s, and *Woman in Billabong*.

Dame Joan Sutherland (1929–) is an operatic soprano who has won praise for her brilliant vocal technique. She is considered one of the greatest singers of all time. She has sung with the world's leading opera companies, usually with her husband, Richard Bonynge, as conductor.

Oodgeroo Noonuccal (formerly Kath Walker) (1920–) is an Aboriginal poet. She is known for her unique style of creating modern works from ancient Aboriginal themes.

Thomas Keneally (1935–) is one of Australia's leading literary figures. He is the author of nineteen novels, including his most famous work, *Schindler's List*. It received England's Booker Prize and has been made into an Academy Award-winning film seen by audiences all over the world.

Sir Sidney Nolan's mysterious painting Glenrowan *was done in the 1950s.*

wrote the book on which the movie was based. He has written many other books as well.

There are so many superb Australian writers that they cannot all be listed. Patrick White, however, must be included. He has an international reputation as one of Australia's best modern writers of fiction.

Famous Films

Most people know of recent Australian movies and their great success. It is interesting to discover that Australia produced a few good silent films, back at the very beginning of movie-making. And the first feature film was made in Australia. This was before Hollywood became the focus of the industry in the early twentieth century.

Australian films have become very popular over the last twenty years. One of the most popular Australian movies ever was *Mad Max*, which starred Mel Gibson. The Australian comedy *Crocodile Dundee*, produced and starred in by Paul Hogan, was enjoyed by millions of people overseas. *Strictly Ballroom*, another Australian movie, delighted audiences around the world.

Popular Music

Some Australian rock groups are known internationally. AC/DC, Air Supply, Little River Band, INXS, and Midnight Oil are some of the most famous. Midnight Oil often performs thought-provoking music. One of its songs, "Beds Are Burning," asks white Australians how they can sleep well at night when the Aborigines have been so badly treated. In this way, the band hopes to have an impact on how people treat one another in the bright Australian future.

Country Facts

Official Name: Commonwealth of Australia

Capital: Canberra

Location: southeast of mainland Asia. The island continent of Australia lies between the Indian Ocean (to the west) and the South Pacific (to the east).

Area: 2,966,150 square miles (7,682,300 square kilometers). *Greatest distances:* north–south: 1,950 miles (3,138 kilometers); east–west: 2,475 miles (3,983 kilometers). *Coastline:* 17,366 miles (27,948 kilometers), including Tasmania and offshore islands

Elevation: *Highest:* Mount Kosciusko, 7,310 feet (2,228 meters) above sea level. *Lowest:* Lake Eyre, 52 feet (16 meters) below sea level

Climate: varies greatly by region. Mostly dry and mild. Some tropical coastal pockets; extreme heat in the desert area in the summer

Population: 18 million; 87 percent urban, 13 percent rural

Form of Government: Constitutional monarchy. Elizabeth II, queen of England, is the head of state. The prime minister is the head of government.

Important Products: *Agriculture:* sheep, wool, cattle, dairy products, wheat, sugarcane, fruit, wine. *Manufactured goods:* processed foods; iron, steel, and other metals; transportation equipment; paper. *Minerals:* bauxite, coal, copper, diamonds, gold, iron ore, lead, manganese, natural gas, nickel, opals, petroleum, silver, tin, tungsten, uranium, zinc.

Basic Unit of Money: Australian dollar; 1 dollar = 100 cents

Language: mainly English; some Aboriginal, European, and Asian languages spoken

Religion: Christianity is the major religion: Protestant (Church of England), 26 percent; Roman Catholic, 26 percent; other Christian faiths, 24 percent. The rest of the people belong to Hindu, Buddhist, Jewish, Muslim, and Aboriginal faiths.

Flag: dark blue background with the red-and-white Union Jack (British flag) in the top left corner. Below is one large white star, for the Commonwealth. To the right are five smaller stars, for the Southern Cross constellation.

National Anthems: "Advance Australia Fair"; "God Save the Queen"

Major Holidays: New Year's Day, January 1; Australia Day, January 26; Good Friday and Easter Monday (dates vary); ANZAC Day, April 25; Queen Elizabeth's birthday (second Monday in June); Christmas Day, December 25; Boxing Day, December 26

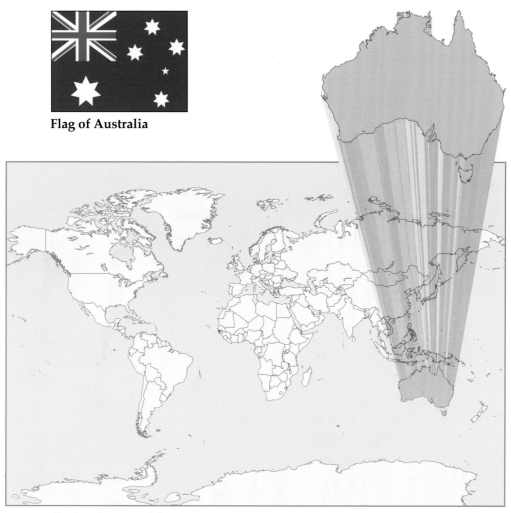

Flag of Australia

Australia in the World

61

Glossary

Aborigines (ah-buh-RI-juh-nees)**:** the first inhabitants of Australia and their descendants

aquaculture: the raising of fish and other sea or lake life for food and other purposes

bush: in Australia, a large area of open, uncultivated land with bushes, low trees, and shrubs; a wilderness

colony: a settlement of people in a new land that is ruled by the government of the country where they came from

corroboree (kuh-RO-buh-ree)**:** a sacred Aboriginal ceremony of music and dance

didgeridoo (dee-jer-ree-DOO): a musical instrument played by Aborigines that makes a wailing sound

dreaming: a trance, or state in which Aborigines believe they communicate with their ancestor spirits

dreamtime: in Aborigine mythology, the time of the world's creation

homestead: a home in the outback; the homestead may be a simple, small house or a larger, more elaborate structure or set of buildings

marsupial: a mammal that has a pouch in which to carry its newborn until it has developed enough to move on its own

outback: the remote, vast, inland region of Australia

transportation: exile in Australia instead of a prison term in England

For Further Reading

Gunner, Emily. *A Family in Australia.* New York: The Bookwright Press, 1985.

Heseltine, Harry, ed. *The Penguin Book of Australian Short Stories.* Ringwood, Australia: Penguin Books, 1990.

Kelly, Andrew. *Australia.* New York: The Bookwright Press, 1989.

McDonald, Jo, and Reven Uihlein. *Australia in Pictures.* Minneapolis, Minnesota: Lerner Publications Company, 1990.

Rajendra, Vejeya and Sundran. *Australia.* Tarrytown, New York: Marshall Cavendish, 1991.

Stark, Al. *Australia: A Lucky Land.* Minneapolis, Minnesota: Dillon Press, 1987.

Index

Page numbers for illustrations are in boldface

About the Author

Jacqueline Drobis Meisel was born in the small gold-mining town of Welkom in the Orange Free State province of South Africa. She graduated from the University of the Witwatersrand in Johannesburg and went on to teach high school.

Ms. Meisel now lives in California with her husband, Alex, and their two sons. She has returned to her native land to research material for articles and books. In 1994, she wrote a book for young adults about the first free elections in her home country. It is entitled *South Africa at the Crossroads*.